Jake's Papers

by Sidney Allen
illustrated by Andy San Diego

Practice Decodable 51

McGraw Hill Education

Bothell, WA • Chicago, IL • Columbus, OH • New York, NY

MHEonline.com

Send all inquiries to:
McGraw-Hill Education
8787 Orion Place
Columbus, OH 43240

ISBN: 978-0-02-138935-3
MHID: 0-02-138935-7

Printed in China.

8 9 10 11 12 DSS 27 26 25 24 23

As Jake ate, the table started shaking!
What was rumbling in the lane?

Jake gazed past the drapes.
Jake spotted flames!

Jake grabbed a stack of papers.
He ran in the yard.

A strong man was at the gate.
"This is more waste," called Jake.

Jake gave his papers to the man.
"Thanks, Jake," said the man.

The man waved. "It is getting late, Jake!"